THE BATTLE OF
THE FROGS AND THE MICE

THE BATTLE OF THE FROGS AND THE MICE

A Homeric Fable

GEORGE W. MARTIN

ILLUSTRATED BY

FRED GWYNNE

JEREMY P. TARCHER/PENGUIN

A member of Penguin Group (USA) Inc.

New York

TARCHER
PENGUIN

JEREMY P. TARCHER/PENGUIN
Published by the Penguin Group
Penguin Group (USA) Inc., 375 Hudson Street,
New York, New York 10014, USA

USA · Canada · UK · Ireland · Australia
New Zealand · India · South Africa · China

Penguin Books Ltd, Registered Offices: 80 Strand, London WC2R 0RL, England
For more information about the Penguin Group visit penguin.com

Originally published 1962 by Dodd, Mead
First Jeremy P. Tarcher/Penguin edition 2013
Copyright © 1962, 1990 by George Martin

Most Tarcher/Penguin books are available at special quantity discounts for
bulk purchase for sales promotions, premiums, fund-raising, and educational
needs. Special books or book excerpts also can be created to fit specific needs.
For details, write Penguin Group (USA) Inc. Special Markets, 375 Hudson Street,
New York, NY 10014.

ISBN 978-0-399-16285-5

Printed in the United States of America
1 3 5 7 9 10 8 6 4 2

This book is printed on acid-free paper.

"But before I praise the dead, I should like to point out by what principles of action we rose to power, and under what institutions and through what manner of life our empire became great."

—PERICLES   (Funeral Oration)

TABLE OF CONTENTS

Samir

EQ: How should we behave?

LET History record: 'Twas Puff-jaw
First the war did start though later
He denied it.

It happened thus:

THE
INCIDENT

ONE day a Mouse, hot and thirsty,
Just from a weasel's jaws escaped,
Crept to the edge of the pond to
Cool his muzzle in the water.

The mouse

   There from a lily-pad Puff-jaw spied
Him and called in such words as these:
"Stranger, who are you? By what right
Do you take water from the Frogs' pond?"

drank from the Frogs pond.

   To which the Mouse, his strength still spent,
Remembering the weasel and
Uncertain of the Frog, replied:

   "Crum-snatcher is my name, son of
Cake-eater, the stout-hearted, and Quern-licker,
Daughter of Ham-gnawer, the King.
In the mouse-hole she bore me and
There nourished me with figs and nuts.
I drink now to slake my thirst as
All creatures must. Nature's law it is,
And Nature the pond provided."

Crum right, its nature pond.

Puff-jaw, observing the Mouse to
Be alone, pushed off from the lily
And with long, slow strokes, so the Mouse
Might admire the strength of his legs,
Stopped just short of the shore and said:

"I am Puff-jaw, King of the Frogs,
Reared by my father, Peleus,
Who mated with Waterlady
On the banks of the Eridanus.
This pond is the Frogs'; the shore, too.
For we have tamed the air and learnt
To leap on land as well as plunge
Beneath the surface of the water.
In return Nature has enlarged
Our realm.

"But drink," he urged, hopping ~~Frog let him drink.~~
Up the bank beside the Mouse.

Crum-snatcher sucked in the water slowly
While he surveyed the Frog whose sleek
Green skin glistened with the water's sheen.
Then raising his head and straightening
His whiskers he observed simply:
"Nature has twice blessed the Frogs
In granting life on land and pond."

Then Puff-jaw answered with a smile:
"No need for caution; I'm your friend
And eager only to exhibit
The many marvels of our realm
Both in the pond and on the shore.
If you would see them, 'tis easily done:
Mount my back, and I will carry you safe."

The Mouse, glancing at the water
Which he disliked and at the Frog
Whom he mistrusted, was about to refuse
When he remembered the sharp-nosed weasel,
Balked and hungry, in the brambles
Behind him. "As I am passing
Your way"—he bowed and without more
Climbed carefully onto the Frog's broad back.

Now at first while he still saw the shore
Near by, Crum-snatcher was pleased,
For there were marvelous sights sufficient
To stupefy a grandchild, and Puff-jaw
Swam easily and well.

But then a horrid
Spectacle appeared, a terror
For both—a water snake thrust its
Freckled neck above the water.

Water
Snake
came.

Puff-jaw, forgetting his helpless
Friend, dove to the bottom and escaped
Black death. But Crum-snatcher, so deserted,
Struggled in vain, sank oft and with
His sprawlings came afloat, breast up,
Hands grasping the air, but the water
Weighting his fur washed over him, and
At the last he cried "Peepe" and perished.
   His death was seen from the shore by
Plate-licker, who, crawling out a log,

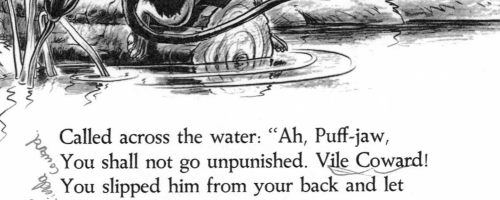

Called across the water: "Ah, Puff-jaw,
You shall not go unpunished. Vile Coward!
You slipped him from your back and let
Him drown like any castaway.

On land you were not the better man.
Heaven and we Mice will punish you."
    Then tearing at his fur so that
Tears spilt from his eyes and piping
"Woe, woe," he ran to tell the Mice
What he had seen.
                    And when they heard
Of Crum-snatcher's brave death and how
Even as they spoke his corpse, face up,
Floated on the pond unable still
To make the safety of the shore,
They were seized with a furious anger

they
mad.

And bade their heralds summon all
To meet at dawn before the hole
Of Cake-eater, the wretched father
Of the ill-fated, ship-wrecked Mouse.

THE COUNCILS
OF WAR AND
THE ARMING

WHEN the Mice in haste had gathered,
Cake-eater, his whiskers wet and drooping,
Addressed the crowd in words like these:
"You all know me: I had three sons.
The first the sniffing weasel killed
Outside the hole. Another died
Of agonizing poison.
Today I lost the last and best,
Crum-snatcher, whom Puff-jaw has carried
Into the deep and drowned. If I
And Quern-licker, a mother thrice-bereft
Of rightful joys and blessings,
If we two alone appear to suffer
From the Frogs, do not be deceived;
They plan some mischief for us all.
They will come, hopping out of the pond,
Smooth-faced and hairless, using their
Front legs merely to rest not to run.
So arm yourselves and follow me,
And we will meet them on the shore."

With such words he persuaded them,
And they began at once to arm.
Those that had swords cleaned and honed them
While telling stories of their battles
Long ago. Others made swords new
From chips of slate, hammering them
Into shape, and though many split
And were lost, enough remained, and these
They blessed by watching through the night.

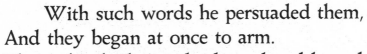

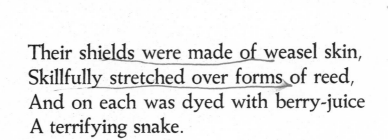

Their shields were made of weasel skin,
Skillfully stretched over forms of reed,
And on each was dyed with berry-juice
A terrifying snake.

The spears
Were of two kinds: the light for far-
Throwing were fashioned from pine-needles,
The heavy, which only the strongest could wield,
Were made of stubble, smoothed and sharpened
To a pitiless point. For their heads
The helmets were of peanut shells.

So the Mice armed, and when the Frogs
Heard of it, they rose from the water
And gathered round the log in council.
And while each asked the other whence
The quarrel rose and why the Mice should arm,
A herald from the Mice drew near,
Pot-searcher, son of great-hearted Cheese-scooper,
Bearing a wand of peace and parley
But speaking thus grim words of war:

"Frogs, pay heed and then take counsel
With yourselves. The Mice have armed and
Send me with their threats to you.
For they have seen the noble Crum-snatcher,
Dead and drifting in the water,
Drowned by your King, Puff-jaw, a vile
And treacherous Frog. So fight then, Frogs,
As many as are warriors
Among you."

At such words the proud Frogs
Croaked and clamored till the log rang.
But some few questioned Puff-jaw,
And to answer these he rose and said:

"Friends, I killed no Mouse. Nor did I
Even see one perish, though like you
I too have seen the dark carcass
Course with the wind across our pond.
I think he drowned while wantoning
Upon our waters, aping us
And practising to swim.

"I swear
I did not see him drown, and yet
These worst of Vermin dare to charge me,
Your King, who am in no way guilty
But am as pure today as when
With spring water you anointed me.
Therefore I urge we arm in answer
To the wily Mice and drench their
Arrogance by driving them along
The shore and into the death-dealing
Waters where Frogs alone survive."

*Puff Jaw
wants
to fight.*

Then up rose Pond-larker, beloved
By some but despised by more for
His quiet manner and reasonable ways.

"Think first," he urged, "that many Mice
Will die; then think again that Frogs,
Not a few, will also perish.
And the pond for many summers
Will be polluted with their rotting
Remains, leaving no cause to sing
Even to those who may survive.
And for what? The death of one Mouse,
Killed, no one knows how for sure.
Better it would be if we drove
The corpse ashore, covered it with

18

A lily-pad and honored it
With a chorus. For this quarrel
Has no cause save choleric blood which
Floods our brains with angry words."
        But the Frogs were not with him, and
Puff-jaw, breaking in, cried aloud:

"This is teatime talk when what we
Need is action, swift and certain,
That leaves its mark, plain, for all to see.
Pollution is a threat but not
As Pond-larker pretends to paint it.
Better to say the danger lies
In letting the Mice approach the pond,
For in their fur they hide disease
And dirt; often they pass poison
Through their bowels. Who knows how this one,
This Crum-snatcher, may have died, or
In what filth he may have frolicked?
But howsoever, his puffy corpse
Already spoils our pond for us.
Therefore I say we arm to drive
Them from the shore and set up there
A trophy to commemorate
Our Victory and their leaving."

    At this all but Pond-larker cried aloud,

And these words the herald, Pot-searcher,
Bore back to the Mice who clanged
Their spears and shields
In answering anger.

Then the Frogs armed, guarding their shins
With skillfully fashioned lily-pads,
And tough cabbage leaves were their shields.
Each had a sharp rush for a spear
And a smooth snail-shell to cover
His head. And as they stood in rank
Along the shore, waving their spears,
Courage filled the heart of each.

THE BATTLE

THEN the Frogs, with a great cry, called
On their Gods and sounded the fell
Note of war, while up the bank each Mouse _wars_
In place knelt by his spear and prayed _starts._
To the God of the Fields for Victory.
Then each side, shrieking, rushed at the other.

Mud-man was the first to fall, speared
Through the chest so hard he fell back
And was pinned to the ground. Pot-searcher,
The herald, was the Mouse that did it;
But Pond-larker saw and struck him
In the belly, right through the mid-riff.
Down he fell on his face, and his
Soft fur filled with degrading dust.
Then Plate-licker smote Loud-croaker so that
His soul soughed from his lips, and by him

A frog fell alright

Died many more with none to know
Their last words. Then the giant Frog,
Cabbage-eater, picked up a large pebble,
Smashed it on Plate-licker's helm
And blood gushed from the Mouse's nose
And ears while his soul flew forth from
His Mouth. Meanwhile Cheese-nibbler hurled
His spear at Puff-jaw, but the aim
Was poor, and before he could recover,
Puff-jaw severed his head with a stroke.

Cheese-nibbler tried to get Puff-jaw.

THE DEATH OF CABBAGE-EATER

AT first the God of War seemed to favor
The Frogs, and the fight flowed against
The Mice who retreated up the bank.
But Troglodyte, a Prince of Mice,
Rallied the despairing and, killing
Two Frogs with one blow, led the charge
Along the bank. Even the giant Frog
Cabbage-eater fled before him, retreating
Down to the water's edge where he
Turned,

T. even scared Cabbage eater

T. killed 2 frogs at once.

but too late. For Troglodyte,
Whirling his sword overhead, slashed
Him from his head to his soft stomach
So that he never more drew in air,
And his sticky blood stained the sand.
He was truly a giant among Frogs,
And as he lay, his fat entrails
(By his small guts' impulsion) broke
Way out at his wound.

T. killed
Cabbage
eater.

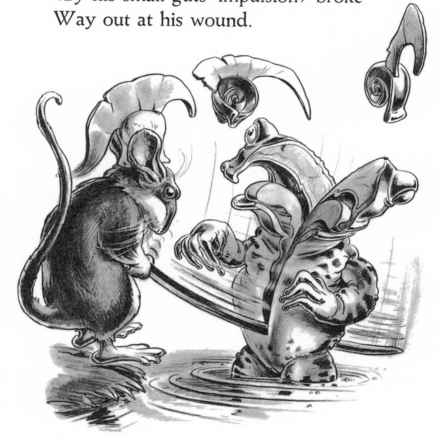

Then were the Frogs
Afraid; some took to the water,
Others hid among the lilies,
Even Puff-jaw crouched irresolute,
His neck-skin quaking in and out,
And with the others looked to Pond-larker,
Standing alone on shore among
The dead.

The
Frogs
were
afraid.

That Frog looked long at them,
At the pond with its tranquil lilies
And the sky reflected in its surface,
Then he turned and, taking the sword
From the limp hand of dead Cabbage-eater,
Called to Troglodyte in these words:

"Great Prince, come. For you or I must
This day die. We cannot both survive."
At these awesome words all other Mice
Save Troglodyte fell back and cleared
A space. High on the bank the old
King, white-whiskered Ham-gnawer, saw his
Son step forward, raised his hand, as
If to stop him, and then let it fall
With a sigh.

Pond-Larken
wants a duel
with T.

POND=LARKER AND
TROGLODYTE

THE two warriors
Faced each other, saluted, then warily
Began to circle. Troglodyte struck first,
A quick thrust at the neck which Pond-larker
Parried even as he slashed at Troglodyte's
Shoulder. But the Mouse was too quick
And leapt from under the blow.
Then the strokes came thick and fast, till
Those around did later swear the
Very ground began to tremble
At the sound. But neither could the other
Scratch; the Mouse was too nimble,
And the Frog, too strong.

So they stopped
To catch a breath, and in that instant
The crowd around began to cry
"Again" and cheered to urge them on.
        "You fight far better than your cause
Deserves," gasped Troglodyte.
Softly Pond-larker replied: "Bad
Causes have only courage to
Recommend them."
                Then grasping his
Sword he struck at Troglodyte who
Warded with his shield, bent double
And thrust up. His sword point scored
Pond-larker's arm, and the bright blood
Sprang out for all to see. The Mice

T. hit
Pond-larker

Cheered, but the Frogs groaned and some
Called Pond-larker "Coward." But he, not
Pausing or protesting, smashed his shield
Against Troglodyte's with such force
The Mouse staggered and only just recovered
To avoid the sword, but even so
His shield lay shattered and his left arm
Hung loosely at his side. Now the advantage
Was Pond-larker's, and the watching Frogs
Clamored for the Mouse's death while
The Mice, fearful, fell silent.
                              But now
          Troglodyte fought more brilliantly
          Than before. Like an angry gnat
          Upon the water he darted

In and out, thrusting, parrying,
And always high so that Pond-larker's
Gored arm grew tired and the Mouse's
Sword began to flick Pond-larker's soft
Throat till it seemed he sweated blood.
     Then Pond-larker stepped back and cried

"A word, a boon." And Troglodyte,
His left arm slapping on his side,
Paused. "Only this," the Frog began,
"When you kill me, let no one speak
Over my body but yourself."
"And thou for me," the Mouse responded.

Then Mice and Frogs around the pair
Cried "Villain," "Traitor" and "He's not
Our kind." But higher on the bank
Troglodyte's father began to weep.
      The two saluted, sighed, stepped back
And crouched again to kill. This time
Pond-larker struck first, a mighty blow
But one which missed its mark, and
Troglodyte returned with a thrust
To the side. Then followed thrust and
Parry, parry, thrust, all so swift
That in a second none could see
Troglodyte's sword cut through the Frog's
Throat to the back bone and the blood
Splashed over the Mouse. But even in that
Instant Pond-larker with a last
Mighty effort of his legs leapt
And fell against Troglodyte, stabbing
Him through the breast. As each fell he
Gripped the other, and they rolled in
An embrace till all their blood was mixed.

Both died.

AFTER THE BATTLE

THE Frogs at once declared they'd won
As also did the Mice. And each
Taking up its warrior carried
His corpse a bit apart to do
Him honor. Then Cake-eater, the father
Of Crum-snatcher, strode forward to speak
Over Troglodyte. But as he started
A murmuring arose in the
Farthest ranks which parted to let
Ham-gnawer, the dead Prince's father,
Pass. Slowly, looking neither to
The right nor to the left, he came
Forward through the crowd till
He stood alone beside his son.
Dry-eyed he stared down at him.

Cake-eater

spoke over

T,

Then carefully he folded the corpse
In his arms and carried it away
Without a word to anyone.
Those who dared, murmured against him
For preferring his private grief
Over their public spectacle.

Down the shore Puff-jaw spoke over
Pond-larker. "We must never forget
Nor let our eyes grow dim nor our hearts
Impervious to this great example of
Pond-larker in battle with the Mice.
From it our children will learn who
Hates the Frogs and is their enemy
And how to deal with him — even,
As Pond-larker has done, unto death.
        For what is life for us Frogs
           If Mice can run along our shore,

Drink of our water and come to our
Councils with arrogant threats of war?
We must make secure our claim to
All the shore and preserve our pond
From pollution by others. — And now
In memory of our own Pond-larker
Let us bare our heads and bow them
In silence for two minutes."

Frogs
honor
Pond-Larker.

                     Each frog
Uncovered and bowed his head. Many wept
While others stood stiff and straight with pride
In their bearing.

               But before the time
                Was passed, it began to rain;

Large drops, singly at first, and then
Pelting, till Frogs and Mice alike
Fled for cover.
                    Till night it rained
And longer as though the soft sand,
Abashed at the stain of blood, had asked
The Heaven to scour it. And on the shore
Alone and in the dark lay Pond-larker
Staring at the Heavens with open eyes
As the driving rain cleansed his corpse
    So on that day ended the Battle
Of the Frogs and Mice.

That   day   the
    war
        ended.